LOBCOCKS
AND
FARTLEBERRIES

summersdale

LOBCOCKS AND FARTLEBERRIES

This selection copyright © Summersdale Publishers Ltd, 2010

Text originally published by S. Hooper, London in 1785 in *A Classical Dictionary of the Vulgar Tongue*, by Francis Grose

Illustrations by David Procter

Summersdale Publishers Ltd
46 West Street
Chichester
West Sussex
PO19 1RP
UK

www.summersdale.com

Printed and bound in the Czech Republic

ISBN: 978-1-84953-101-6

Substantial discounts on bulk quantities of Summersdale books are available to corporations, professional associations and other organisations. For details contact Summersdale Publishers by telephone: +44 (0) 1243 771107, fax: +44 (0) 1243 786300 or email: nicky@summersdale.com.

LOBCOCKS

AND

FARTLEBERRIES

18TH-CENTURY INSULTS TO CONFOUND YOUR FOES

Illustrations by David Procter

FRANCIS GROSE

INTRODUCTION

Welcome, aspiring vulgarites, to *Lobcocks and Fartleberries*, an ingenious and indecorous collection of insults derived from the work of the original connoisseur of curse words, Francis Grose. His dictionary of eighteenth-century vernacular, *The Vulgar Tongue*, was published in London in 1785, collecting for the first time many of the familiar 'cant' (slang) and 'burlesque' (parodic) terms of the age.

Here you will find a choice selection of the most colourful and confounding of these colloquialisms, along with a few more everyday terms that will help you compose an impressive array of devilish retorts.

So, for those of you who wish to sharpen your tongue and revel in some sophisticated slandering, ready your 'poxy ogles' and 'grubby fams', and prepare your 'idea pot' for a short, sharp kick in the 'inexpressibles'!

A NOTE ABOUT THE TEXT

In an effort to retain some of the characteristic cadences of the eighteenth-century vernacular found in Grose's original book, the editor has left unchanged a number of orthographical curiosities and archaisms that appear in his 1785 edition.

ADDLE PLOT

A spoil-sport, a mar-all.

ALE DRAPER

An alehouse keeper.

ALTITUDES

The man is in his altitudes, i.e. he is drunk.

AMBIDEXTER

A lawyer who takes fees from both plaintiff and defendant, or both parties in gaming.

ANGLING FOR FARTHINGS

Begging out of a prison window with a cap, or box, let down at the end of a long string.

APE LEADER

An old maid: their punishment after death
for neglecting to increase and multiply
will be, it is said, leading apes in hell.

APPLE DUMPLIN SHOP

A woman's bosom.

ARCH DUKE

A comical or eccentric fellow.

ARS MUSICA

A bumfiddle; the backside.

ARSY VARSEY

To fall arsy varsey, i.e. head over heels.

ATHANASIAN WENCH

A forward girl, ready to oblige
every man that shall ask her.

BACON-FACED

Full-faced.

BANTLING

A young child.

'Have you ever clapped eyes on such a wizened THORNBACK? There's nought but a couple of rotten apples left in the DUMPLIN SHOP of that wrinkly MOPSQUEEZER.'

THORNBACK: An old maid.
APPLE DUMPLIN SHOP: A woman's bosom.
MOPSQUEEZER: A maid servant; particularly a house maid.

BEARD-SPLITTER

A man much given to wenching.

BEETLE-BROWED

One having thick projecting eyebrows.

BETWATTLED

Surprised, confounded, out of
one's senses; also bewrayed.

BIDDY, or CHICK-A-BIDDY

A chicken and, figuratively, a young wench.

BITCH BOOBY

A country wench.

BONE BOX

The mouth. Shut your bone box;
shut your mouth.

TO BOX THE JESUIT
A sea term for masturbation.

BRACKET-FACED

Ugly, hard-featured.

BULLY BACK

A bully to a bawdy-house; one who is kept in
pay to oblige the frequenters of the house
to submit to the impositions of
the mother abbess, or bawd.

BUMFIDDLE

The backside; the breech.

BUNG NIPPER

A cut-purse.

BUTTOCK BROKER

A bawd, or match-maker.

CAT STICKS

Thin legs, compared to sticks
with which boys play at 'cat'.*

CATCH FART

A footboy; so called from such servants
commonly following close behind
their master or mistress.

* An eighteenth-century game involving a metre-long stick used to
flick up and strike a shorter stick as far as possible.

CHEESE TOASTER

A sword.

TO CHOUSE

To cheat or trick; he choused me out of it.

CLACK

A tongue, chiefly applied to women; a simile
drawn from the clack of a water-mill.

'Away with you BANTLING, before ye catch a swift clip to the back of your CAT STICKS! Fed with a FIRESHOVEL were ye, you pestering POWDER MONKEY? And what crusty elephant LUGS!'

BANTLING: A young child.

CAT STICKS: Thin legs, compared to sticks with which boys play at cat.

FIRESHOVEL: He or she, when young, was fed with a fire shovel; a saying of persons with wide mouths.

POWDER MONKEY: A boy on board a ship of war, whose business it is to fetch powder from the magazine.

LUGS: Ears, or wattles.

CLOAK TWITCHERS

Rogues who lurk about the entrance into dark
alleys and bye-lanes to snatch cloaks from
the shoulders of passengers.

COCK ROBIN

A soft, easy fellow.

COLLAR DAY

Execution day.

CORNEY-FACED

A very red, pimpled face.

CRAB LANTHORN

A peevish fellow.

CRACKER

Crust, sea biscuit or ammunition loaf; also the backside. Farting crackers; breeches.

CRUMP-BACKED

Hump-backed.

CRUSTY BEAU

One that uses paint and cosmetics
to obtain a fine complexion.

CULLY

A fop or fool; also, a dupe to women; from
the Italian word *coglione*, a blockhead.

DAY LIGHTS

Eyes. To darken his day lights or sew up his
eyes; to close up a man's eyes in boxing.

DANDY PRAT

An insignificant or trifling fellow.

DEVIL DRIVER

A parson.

DING

To knock down. To ding it in one's ears; to
reproach or tell someone something
one is not desirous of hearing.

DISHCLOUT

A dirty, greasy woman. He has made a napkin of
his dishclout; a saying of one who
has married his cook maid.

DOGGESS, DOG'S WIFE

Jocular way of calling a woman a bitch.

DOODLE SACK

A bagpipe. Also the
private parts of a woman.

DOWSE ON THE CHOPS

A blow to the face.

'There's a HATCHET-FACED CLOAK TWITCHER if ever I saw one – those darkened DAY LIGHTS make him look slyer than OLD SCRATCH himself. No doubt he's escaped a COLLAR DAY or two in his time.'

HATCHET-FACED: A long, thin face.

CLOAK TWITCHER: Rogues who lurk about the entrance into dark alleys and bye-lanes to snatch cloaks from the shoulders of passengers.

DAY LIGHTS: Eyes. To darken his day lights or sew up his eyes; to close up a man's eyes in boxing.

OLD SCRATCH: The Devil.

COLLAR DAY: Execution day.

DOXIES

She-beggars, wenches, whores.

TO DRUB

To beat anyone with a stick or rope's end;
perhaps a contraction of *dry rub*. It is also used to
signify a good beating with any instrument.

DRY BOOTS

A sly, humorous fellow.

ELBOW SHAKER

A gamester, one who rattles
St Hugh's bones, i.e. the dice.

ENSIGN BEARER

A drunken man,
who looks red in the face.

ERIFFS

Rogues just initiated and
beginning to practise.

ETERNITY BOX

A coffin.

EVES DROPPER

One that lurks about to rob hen-roosts;
also a person who listens at doors and
windows to hear private conversations.

FAMS, FAMBLES

Hands.

FARTLEBERRIES

Excrement hanging about the anus.

FIDDLE FADDLE

Trifling discourse; nonsense. A mere
fiddle faddle fellow; a trifler.

FIRE SHIP

A wench who has the venereal disease.

FIRESHOVEL

He or she, when young, was fed with a fire
shovel; a saying of persons with wide mouths.

FLAP DRAGON

A clap or pox.

FLAYBOTTOMIST

A bum-brusher or schoolmaster.

FLUSTERED

Drunk.

'HOP THE TWIG you poxy BUNG NIPPER, before I have you and your fidgeting FAMBLES hauled away in SHERIFF'S BRACELETS and shut in a cell with only the sound of your stinking ARS MUSICA and a rancid REMEDY CRITCH for company!'

HOP THE TWIG: To run away.
BUNG NIPPER: A cut-purse.
FAMBLES: Hands.
SHERIFF'S BRACELETS: Handcuffs.
ARS MUSICA: A bumfiddle; the backside.
REMEDY CRITCH: A chamber pot or member mug.

FRIBBLE

An effeminate fop; a name borrowed from a celebrated character of that kind in the farce of *Miss in Her Teens*, written by Mister Garrick.

FRUMMAGEMMED

Choked, strangled or hanged.

FUBSEY

Plump. A fubsey wench;
a plump, healthy wench.

GAP STOPPER

A whoremaster.

GARRET

The head. His garret is empty or unfurnished,
i.e. he has no brains, he is a fool.

GIGG

A nose. Grunter's gigg; a hog's snout.
Gigg is also a high one-horse chaise,
and a woman's privities.

GILFLURT

A proud minx; a vain, capricious woman.

GIMBLET-EYED

A person with a squint.

GINGAMABOBS

Toys, bawbles; also a man's testicles.

GIRDS

Quips, taunts, severe or biting reflections.

GOLLUMPUS

A large, clumsy fellow.

GOOSEBERRY-EYED

One with dull grey eyes,
like boiled gooseberries.

GOTCH-GUTTED

Pot-bellied: a gotch, in Norfolk signifying
a pitcher or large round jug.

GROG-BLOSSOM

A carbuncle or pimple in the face,
caused by drinking.

HANG IN CHAINS

A vile, desperate fellow.

HANKTELO

A silly fellow.

'My good man, isn't it time you powdered that PISS-BURNED PERRIWINKLE of yours? What with those grimy VAMPERS, you're beginning to take on the aspect of a first-rate SHABBAROON.'

PISS-BURNED: Discoloured; commonly applied to a discoloured grey wig.
PERRIWINKLE: A wig.
VAMPERS: Stockings.
SHABBAROON: An ill-dressed, shabby fellow; also a mean-spirited person.

HARRIDAN

A hagged [*sic*] old woman; a miserable, scraggy,
worn-out harlot, fit to take her bawd's degree.
Derived from the French word *haridelle*,
a worn-out jade of a horse or mare.

HASH

To flash the hash; to vomit.

HATCHET-FACED

A long, thin face.

HECTOR

A bully, a swaggering coward. To hector; to
bully; probably from such persons affecting
the valour of Hector, the Trojan hero.

HEDGE WHORE

An itinerant harlot who bilks the bagnios and
bawdy-houses, by disposing of her favours
on the way-side, under a hedge; a
low, beggarly prostitute.

HELL-BORN BABE

A lewd, graceless youth; one naturally
of a wicked disposition.

HELL CAT

A termagant; a vixen; a furious,
scolding woman.

HERRING POND

The sea. To cross the herring pond at the
king's expense; to be transported.

HOBBLEDYGEE

A pace between a walk and a run; a dog-trot.

HODDY DODDY, ALL ARSE AND NO BODY

A short clumsy person.

HOPPER-ARSED

Having large projecting buttocks; from their resemblance to a small basket, called a hopper.

HOP THE TWIG

To run away.

IDEA POT

The knowledge box; the head.

INDORSER

A sodomite. To indorse with a cudgel; to drub
or beat a man over the back with a stick;
to lay *cane* upon Abel.

INEXPRESSIBLES

Breeches.

IRISH EVIDENCE

A false witness.

IVY BUSH

Like an owl in an ivy bush; a simile for a meagre
or weasel-faced man with a large wig
or very bushy hair.

'Stand by, here comes the village
DANDY PRAT, the great galloping
GOLLUMPUS. By the look of his half-
arsed HOBBLEDYGEE he's about
to fall ARSY VARSEY.'

DANDY PRAT: An insignificant or trifling fellow.
GOLLUMPUS: A large, clumsy fellow.
HOBBLEDYGEE: A pace between a walk and a run; a dog-trot.
ARSY VARSEY: To fall arsy varsey, i.e. head over heels.

JACK NASTY FACE

A sea term, signifying a common sailor.

JACK SPRAT

A dwarf or diminutive fellow.

JACKANAPES

An ape; a pert, ugly little fellow.

JACK WEIGHT

A fat man.

JACK WHORE

A large, masculine, overgrown wench.

JERRY SNEAK

A henpecked husband; from a celebrated
character in one of Mr Foote's plays,
representing a man governed by his wife.

JINGLE BRAINS

A wild, thoughtless, rattling fellow.

JOCK, or CROWDY-HEADED JOCK

A jeering appellation for a north-country
seaman, particularly a collier; Jock being a
common name of the lower order of the
people in Northumberland.

TO JOCK, or JOCKUM CLOY

To enjoy a woman.

JOHNNY BUM

A jack ass; so called by a lady that affected to be
extremely polite and modest, who would not
say jack because it was vulgar, nor
ass because it was indecent.

JOLTER HEAD

A large head; metaphorically, a stupid fellow.

KEELHAULING

A punishment in use among the Dutch seamen
in which, for certain offences, the delinquent
is drawn once or more under the ship's keel;
ludicrously defined, undergoing
a great hard-ship.

KETTLE DRUMS

Cupid's kettle drums; a woman's breasts.

KICKERAPOO

Dead.

TO KIMBAW

To trick, cheat or cozen; also to beat or to bully.
Let's kimbaw the cull; let's bully the fellow.

KING'S BAD BARGAIN

One of the king's bad bargains; a malingerer
or soldier who shirks his duty.

'There goes another JACK NASTY FACE off to the NANNY HOUSE to find himself a BUTTOCK BROKER. By the looks of his greasy MUZZLE he's seen many a month fetching his own METTLE out on the HERRING POND.'

JACK NASTY FACE: A sea term, signifying a common sailor.
NANNY HOUSE: A brothel.
BUTTOCK BROKER: A bawd or match-maker.
MUZZLE: A beard.
METTLE: The semen. To fetch mettle; the act of self-pollution. Mettle is also figuratively used for courage.
HERRING POND: The sea. To cross the herring pond at the king's expense; to be transported.

KISS MINE ARSE

A kiss mine arse fellow; a sycophant.

KITTLE-PITCHERING

A jocular method of hobbling, or bothering
a troublesome teller of long stories.

KNIGHT AND BARROW PIG

More hog than gentleman. A saying of
any low pretender to precedency.

LACED MUTTON

A prostitute.

LADYBIRDS

Lewd women.

LETCH

A whim of the amorous kind,
out of the common way.

LICKSPITTLE

A parasite, or talebearer.

LOBCOCK

A large, relaxed penis;
also a dull, inanimate fellow.

LONG MEG

A jeering name for a very tall woman: from one
famous story called *Long Meg of Westminster*.

LOOBY

An awkward, ignorant fellow.

LORD

A crooked or hump-backed man.

LUGS

Ears or wattles.

LUMPING

Great. A lumping pennyworth; a great quantity
for the money, a bargain. He has got a lumping
pennyworth; frequently said of a man
who marries a fat woman.

LURCHER

A lurcher of the law; a bum-bailiff or his setter.

MACKEREL

A bawd: from the French *maquerel*.

MADGE

The private parts of a woman.

'What a fine and fertile FUBSEY we have here! BITCH BOOBY or not, I'll disbelieve any man who would deny the urge to polish the KETTLE DRUMS of that young CHICK-A-BIDDY.'

FUBSEY: Plump. A fubsey wench; a plump, healthy wench.
BITCH BOOBY: A country wench.
KETTLE DRUMS: Cupid's kettle drums; a woman's breasts.
BIDDY, or CHICK-A-BIDDY: A chicken and, figuratively, a young wench.

MALKINTRASH

One in a dismal garb.

MERRY-BEGOTTEN

A bastard.

METTLE

The semen. To fetch mettle; the act of self-
pollution. Mettle is also figuratively
used for courage.

MOPSEY

A dowdy or homely woman.

MOPSQUEEZER

A maid servant; particularly a house maid.

MUCKWORM.

A miser.

MUD

A fool or thick-skull'd fellow.

MUTTON MONGER

A man addicted to wenching.

MUZZLE

A beard.

NANNY HOUSE

A brothel.

NATTY LADS

Young thieves or pickpockets.

NETTLED

He or she has pissed on a nettle; said of
one who is peevish or out of temper.

NAZY

Drunken. Nazy cove or mort:
a drunken rogue or harlot.

NICKUMPOOP, or NINCUMPOOP

A foolish fellow; also one who
never saw his wife's privities.

NIGIT

A fool: seemingly a corruption and
contraction of the words *an idiot*.

NOCKY BOY

A dull, simple fellow.

NORFOLK DUMPLING

A nickname, or term of jocular reproach to
a Norfolk man; dumplings being a
favourite food in that county.

'By Gad, if that isn't the most dismal
DOXY I've ever laid eyes upon – schooled
by the ALE DRAPER I suspect, judging by
that hefty GROG-BLOSSOM sprouting
from her grimy NOZZLE.'

DOXIES: She-beggars, wenches, whores.
ALE DRAPER: An alehouse keeper.
GROG-BLOSSOM: A carbuncle or pimple in the face caused
by drinking.
NOZZLE: The nose of a man or woman.

NOTCH

The private parts of a woman.

NOZZLE

The nose of a man or woman.

NUTMEGS

Testicles.

OGLES

Eyes. Rum ogles; fine eyes.

OIL OF GLADNESS

I will anoint you with the oil of gladness;
ironically spoken for, I will beat you.

OLD SCRATCH

The Devil.

OTTOMISED

To be ottomised; to be dissected. You'll be
scragged, ottomised and grin in a glass case;
you'll be hanged, anatomised and your skeleton
kept in a glass case at Surgeons' Hall.

OUTRUN THE CONSTABLE

A man who has lived above his means or
income is said to have outrun the constable.

PACKTHREAD

To talk packthread; to use indecent language
well wrapped up.

PAPER SKULL

A thin-skull'd, foolish fellow.

PEAL

To ring a peal in a man's ears; to scold at him:
his wife rang him such a peal!

PEPPERED

To be infected with venereal disease.

PERRIWINKLE

A wig.

PETTICOAT HOLD

One who has an estate during his wife's
life, called the apron-string hold.

PETTYFOGGER

A dirty little attorney, ready to undertake
any litigious or bad cause.

PICKLE

A waggish fellow. There are rods in brine
or pickle for him; a punishment awaits
him or is prepared for him.

'Take your grimy FAMS off me you
BACON-FACED BULLY BACK, before
I give you a DRUBBING that will put
cracks in your IDEA POT and shake
the FARTLEBERRIES from
your stinking BUMFIDDLE!'

FAMS, FAMBLES: Hands.
BACON-FACED: Full-faced.
BULLY BACK: A bully to a bawdy-house.
TO DRUB: To beat anyone with a stick or rope's end.
IDEA POT: The knowledge box; the head.
FARTLEBERRIES: Excrement hanging about the anus.
BUMFIDDLE: The backside; the breech.

TO PIKE

To run away. Pike off; run away.

PIMP WHISKIN

A top trader in pimping.

PISS-BURNED

Discoloured; commonly applied
to a discoloured grey wig.

PISS-PROUD

Having a false erection. That old fellow thought
he had an erection, but he was only
piss-proud; said of any old fellow who
marries a young wife.

PLUG TAIL

A man's penis.

POWDER MONKEY

A boy on board a ship of war, whose business it
is to fetch powder from the magazine.

QUACK

An ungraduated, ignorant pretender
to skill in physic.

QUEAN

A slut; a worthless woman; a strumpet.

QUEEN STREET

A man governed by his wife is said to live
in Queen Street or at the sign of
the Queen's Head.

QUEER AS DICK'S HATBAND

Out of order, without knowing one's disease.

QUEER BITCH

An odd, out-of-the-way fellow.

QUEER MORT

A diseased strumpet.

QUILL DRIVER

A clerk, scribe or hackney writer.

QUIM

The private parts of a woman; perhaps
from the Spanish *quemar*, to burn.

RACKABACK

A monster with six eyes, three mouths, four arms and eight legs: five on one side and three on the other.

RAGAMUFFIN

A ragged fellow, one all in tatters.

'Any more FIDDLE FADDLE and I'll
put you in your ETERNITY BOX... you
BEARD-SPLITTING CATCH FART!'

FIDDLE FADDLE: Trifling discourse; nonsense. A mere fiddle
faddle fellow; a trifler.
ETERNITY BOX: A coffin.
BEARD-SPLITTER: A man much given to wenching.
CATCH FART: A footboy; so called from such servants
commonly following close behind their master or mistress.

RAG WATER

Gin or any other common dram; these
liquors seldom failing to reduce those
that drink them to rags.

RAILS

A dish of rails; a lecture or scolding from
a married woman to her husband.

RANTALLION

One whose scrotum is so relaxed as to be longer
than his penis, i.e. whose shot pouch is
longer than the barrel of his piece.

RANTIPOLE

A rude romping boy or girl; also a
gadabout dissipated woman.

TO RAP

To take a false oath; also to curse. He rapped out
a volley, i.e. he swore a whole volley of oaths.

RATTLE-PATE

A volatile, unsteady or whimsical
man or woman.

REMEDY CRITCH

A chamber pot or member mug.

RIBALDRY

Vulgar abusive language, such as was spoken
by ribalds. Ribalds were originally mercenary
soldiers who travelled about serving any master
for pay, but afterwards degenerated
into a mere bandit.

TO RIBROAST

To beat. I'll ribroast him to his heart's content.

ROSY GILLS

One with a sanguine or
fresh-coloured countenance.

RUM CULL

A rich fool easily cheated,
particularly by his mistress.

RUSTY GUTS

A blunt, surly fellow: a jocular
misnomer of *rusticus*.

Ss

SAD DOG

A wicked, debauched fellow: one of the ancient
family of the sad dogs. Swift translates it
into Latin by the words *tristis canis*.

SALT

Lecherous. A salt bitch; a bitch on heat, or
proud bitch. Salt eel; a rope's end used to
correct boys, etc. at sea: you shall have
a salt eel for supper.

SATYR

A libidinous fellow.

SAUNTERER

An idle, lounging fellow: by some derived from
sans terre; applied to persons who, having no
lands or home, lingered and loitered about.

SCAB

A worthless person.

'Hold your galloping CLACK you
BEETLE-BROWED BOOB, else I'll splice
your GINGAMABOBS with one swift nick
of my CHEESE TOASTER!'

CLACK: A tongue, chiefly applied to women; a simile drawn
from the clack of a water-mill.
BEETLE-BROWED: One having thick projecting eyebrows.
GINGAMABOBS: Toys, bawbles; also a man's testicles.
CHEESE TOASTER: A sword.

SCAPEGRACE

A wild, dissolute fellow.

SCOTCH FIDDLE

The itch.

SCOURERS

Riotous bucks who amuse themselves with
breaking windows and assaulting every person
they meet: called scouring the streets.

SCRATCH

Old Scratch; the Devil: probably from the
long and sharp claws with which he
is frequently delineated.

SCREW JAWS

A wry-mouthed person.

SHABBAROON

An ill-dressed shabby fellow;
also a mean-spirited person.

SHANKER

A venereal wart.

SHERRIF'S BRACELETS

Handcuffs.

SHITTNG THROUGH THE TEETH.

Vomiting. Hark ye, friend, have you got a
padlock on your arse that you shite through
your teeth? Vulgar address to one vomiting.

SNEAKSBY

A mean-spirited fellow; a sneaking cur.

SOSS BRANGLE

A slatternly wench.

TO SPIFLICATE

To confound, silence or dumbfound.

TABBY

An old maid; either from Tabitha, a formal
antiquated name; or else from a tabby cat,
as old maids are often compared to cats.

TANTADLIN TART

A sirreverence; human excrement.

TEARS OF THE TANKARD

The drippings of liquor on a man's waistcoat.

TENDER PARNELL

A tender creature, fearful of the least
puff of wind or drop of rain.

THATCH-GALLOWS

A rogue or man of bad character.

'That BRACKET-FACED old MUCKWORM looks like an OWL IN AN IVY BUSH and QUEER AS DICK'S HATBAND - it's enough to make you FLASH THE HASH all spontaneous.'

BRACKET-FACED: Ugly, hard-featured.

MUCKWORM: A miser.

IVY BUSH: Like an owl in an ivy bush; a simile for a meagre or weasel-faced man, with a large wig or very bushy hair.

QUEER AS DICK'S HATBAND: Out of order, without knowing one's disease.

HASH: To flash the hash; to vomit.

THINGUMBOB

Mr Thingumbob; a vulgar address or
nomination to any person whose name is
unknown, the same as Mr What-d'ye-call-'em.
Thingumbobs; testicles.

THORNBACK

An old maid.

TIMBER TOE

A man with a wooden leg.

TIPPLERS

Sots, who are continually sipping.

TOAD EATER

A poor female relation; a humble companion or reduced gentlewoman; the standing butt on whom all kinds of practical jokes are played off.

TOSS POT

A drunkard.

TONY

A silly fellow or ninny.
A mere tony; a simpleton.

TOTTY-HEADED

Giddy, hair-brained.

TROTTERS

Feet.

TRUG

A dirty puzzle; an ordinary, sorry woman.

TUFT HUNTER

A university parasite; one who courts the
acquaintance of nobility, whose caps are
adorned with a gold tuft.

TWIDDLE-POOP

An effeminate-looking fellow.

UNDERSTRAPPER

An inferior in any office or department.

UNLICKED CUB

A rude, uncouth young fellow.

UNWASHED BAWDRY

Rank bawdry.

UPPISH

Testy, apt to take offence.

UPSTARTS

Persons lately raised to honours and
riches from mean stations.

'Here comes a CORNEY-FACED DEVIL DRIVER – he's had more than his fair share of RAG WATER judging by his ROSY GILLS and soggy CRACKERS.'

CORNEY-FACED: A very red, pimpled face.

DEVIL DRIVER: A parson.

RAG WATER: Gin or any other common dram; these liquors seldom failing to reduce those that drink them to rags.

ROSY GILLS: One with a sanguine or fresh-coloured countenance.

CRACKER: Crust, sea biscuit or ammunition loaf; also the backside. Farting crackers; breeches.

VAIN-GLORIOUS

One who boasts without reason, or, as the canters say, pisses more than he drinks.

VAMPERS

Stockings.

VAN-NECK

Miss or Mrs Van-neck; a woman
with large breasts.

VARLETS

Now rogues and rascals, formerly
yeomen's servants.

VICE ADMIRAL OF
THE NARROW SEAS

A drunken man that pisses under the
table into his companions' shoes.

WAG

An arch frolicsome fellow.

WAGTAIL

A lewd woman.

WASP

An infected prostitute who, like
a wasp, carries a sting in her tail.

WATER SCRIGER

A doctor who prescribes from inspecting
the water of his patients.

WEASEL-FACED

Thin, meagre-faced. Weasel-gutted;
thin-bodied.

WESTMINSTER WEDDING

A match between a whore and a rogue.

WHAPPER

A large person.

WHELP

An impudent whelp; a saucy boy.

WHIDDLER

An informer or one that betrays
the secrets of gangs.

WHIPPER-SNAPPER

A diminutive fellow.

WHITE FEATHER

He has a white feather; he is a coward:
an allusion to a game cock, where
having a white feather is a proof he
is not of the true game breed.

'Look at that GOTCH-GUTTED JACK WEIGHT! If he were any more HOPPER-ARSED his INEXPRESSIBLES would be in danger of tearing.'

GOTCH-GUTTED: Pot-bellied: a gotch, in Norfolk signifying a pitcher, or large round jug.
JACK WEIGHT: A fat man.
HOPPER-ARSED: Having large projecting buttocks; from their resemblance to a small basket, called a hopper.
INEXPRESSIBLES: Breeches.

YANKEY, or YANKEY DOODLE.

A booby, or country lout: a name given to the
New England men in North America.

YORKSHIRE TYKE

A Yorkshire clown. To come Yorkshire over any
one: to cheat him.

ZAD

Crooked like the letter Z. He is a mere zad,
or perhaps zed; a description of a very
crooked or deformed person.

ZOUCH

A slovenly, un-genteel man; one who has a
stoop in his gait. A slouched hat; a hat with its
brims let down or un-cocked.

Have you enjoyed this book?

If so, why not write a review
on your favourite website?

Thanks very much for buying
this Summersdale book.

www.summersdale.com